bound

Tawny Folk

bound
Copyright © 2020 by Tawny Folk

Soft Cover — 978-1-64318-062-5

Imperium Publishing
1097 N. 400th Rd
Baldwin City, KS, 66006

www.imperiumpublishing.com

for the younger version of me who was always
terrified that someone might read her poetry

special thank you to
jarrett, chloe, leo, benjamin & james

You said if I gave you a little bit of myself
It would inspire you to get help

So I reached in deep
Took important pieces of me
Gladly gave them to you

"I still feel empty"
You moaned through chapped lips
"What else do you have to offer?"
You cried when you were asking me

My only job was to ease your pain

So I reached inside again
Sacrificed some more pieces of my soul

You shook your head, unsatisfied

I couldn't believe how broken you were
And I knew it was my duty to put you back together

Slowly I removed chunks of myself
In hopes to make you whole
So unaware
That I was disappearing

You drained me
In hopes of finding clarity
And then discarded all I gave

You never intended to be
A better version of yourself
You just needed me
To be as broken

◇◇◇◇◇◇◇◇

If you give a narcissist a coy smile
He's going to want your phone number
And if you give him your phone number
He's going to want you to know you're special
And once he tells you that you're special
He's going to convince you that you're the one
And once you think that you're the one
You're going to give him everything he demands

If you give a narcissist everything he demands
He's going to take it without hesitation
(While he convinces you he deserves it
And berates you for being so giving)
And once he has you drained
He's going to tell you how useless you are
And once you feel useless
You're going to want to prove your love
And in order to prove your love
You have to give a little more
And in order to give a little more
You have to give up your confidence
If you give a narcissist your confidence
He'll let you know how weak you are
And once you think you're weak
You'll have to prove that you are strong
You'll have to surrender completely
And once you surrender
He is going to leave
Because he can't possibly love someone
Who has so little to offer

If you give a narcissist a smile
He's going to take your soul

My life
Was
Darkness ahead
Darkness behind
You are the light
I was destined to find
But by the time I arrived
You had begun to burn out
Flickering
I saw you in the distance
I thought refuge was close by
Little did I know
I had been glowing the whole time
And you lured me in,
Hardly lit
So you could take my shine

I feel so
Out of control
As if you've possessed me
In every single way
I sit and cry hoping if I sob enough
You'll leak right out of my body
And the urge to get a reaction out of you
Wont haunt me anymore
I imagine you're like something foul I ingested
Wish I could reach down my throat
And purge you out
Rid of you
Rid of this pain
I need you out of my soul

The delusion is unreal
Standing on a pedestal
You built from trash and dirt
Yelling obscenities
At all of those you have hurt
Preaching to them from your cage
About the wars you have braved
So proud of yourself
For making it through
Oblivious to the fact
That life is moving on around you
And you're not the leader you think you are
They are not scattering after heeding your advice
They are acknowledging your madness
And running for their lives
It amazes me
How you put a hand to everything
And claim it as a creation of your own
Yet you're locked into a life of emptiness
And you're nothing
Except alone

I don't miss you when you're gone
I just love the chaos
It's all I know
I have never been loved
Without condition
The possibility of rejection
Has always loomed
In all my relationships

I was abandoned before I knew what love was
So now it can't exist without pain

mislead

I would gladly follow you into the darkness
Which I think
Is a testament of my love
But the fact that you
Would lead me there
Makes me questions yours

Your return was bittersweet

To hear you admit that you made a mistake
That was the validation I always craved

But realizing I never really loved you scares me
Because I know that if you had never left
I probably would've stayed

Trying to heal from trauma

With someone who caused my trauma

While they try to heal from their trauma

And they trauma they caused me

Our lives running in circles

The same fights over and over again

Whoever hits harder must love more

But whoever loves more, loses

Can't be with you

Can't be without you

Can't be kind

Can't keep fighting

We both lose

I wake up needing you

Dreaming so hard I can feel you

Open my eyes and it's not the real you

Just my imagination

I wake up hating you
Trying to block you out of my mind
But I cant fight off the urge
To tell you how much I hate you
Suddenly, screaming seems fine
As long as I'm getting your attention

Sometimes I swear
We're going to get better
Everything, we'll change
And we'll love just fine
But sometimes I swear
I live in a fantasy
Nothing can change
It'll never feel right

And the history repeats itself
The good and the bad
My heart aches at random
You're the worst
And the best
That I've ever had

A little bit each day
I feel the love draining out
Feel the ache going away
A little bit each day

I wish I could cry it all out in one shot
Binge on the memories
Purge out the tears
And be done with it
Be done with you
Never look back
Never second guess
Never let my kindness disguise itself as weakness

But instead I have to feel it
A little bit each day
I have to hope that I'll miss you less
And let go a little more
But even these hopes change
A little bit each day

I can't love you
And love myself
At the same time

Someone always loses

Either I love you completely
And I live my life drained
Longing
Feeling like something is missing

Or I look inward
And I decide to love me
And I leave you
Completely

And I think both of our characters are explained
During this push and pull
The idea that I'd pick you as the winner
Says so much about who I could be
But the fact that you'd let me be the loser
Makes it clear that neither of us
Actually loves me

It's scary
Unnerving
The way we treat each other
How quick we are to snap
But there's sick pleasure in knowing
I can be my ugliest self – possible
And you still come back

I have been so very careful
My whole life
About using the word soulmate
I have waited and waited
For the earth to shake under me
The wind to be knocked out of me
While feeling more comfortable
Then I ever have in my life
And then there was you
My soulmate

So strong, so sure
Having never felt it before
Only to find out that you
Had been throwing the word around so loosely
And so many pieces of your past
Out to let me know that we're doomed to fail
Letting me know they were your soulmate first

And I guess I can't be mad
Maybe you thought so
And you just happened to be wrong
But maybe, just maybe
You're wrong about me too
And you're just loose with your words

The dark place
That's what I call it when my brain takes over
It gets cloudy
And all I can focus on is the pain
And I obsess over the idea
That the light will never shine again
I can't see beyond the fog
Because I'm sucked in completely
The dark place

For so long I thought
That you could be the sun
That no darkness could consume me
Because you'd be illuminated
At all times
And you'd keep me tucked safely inside
"no more dark places" I thought
Wow, what a concept

16 months
That's how long I've claimed to love
And you have claimed to love me back
"from the very first moment" we'd say
As if we always knew
And sometimes I think we really did
Sometimes I swear we're a perfect fit
But then sometimes
An eclipse
Everything else in the world becomes more important
Than keeping me in the sunshine

The dark place …& you
I realize now they're synonyms
And you were never the sun

We were sitting where the water splashes the rocks
and just barely brushes your skin
When you told me you weren't going anywhere, ever
With an outstretched hand you promised
You would always love me
Whether times were bad or great
Even when I couldn't get myself together
I'd have someone

We were dancing in the room you built
When you sang to her
Begged her to come back home
and for once you didn't get mad when anyone cried
With a strong embrace and a smiley face
You promised everything would be okay

We were standing at the top of the steps
When we were sure that everything had changed
and you admitted in all your rage
Life would've been easier if we hadn't of stayed
as badly as I wanted to reject everything you said
I believed every word, I cracked under every thought
I was begging for life when I stopped loving you

But you know, you're never gone
and I will never mind
It's the honest truth when I say
You have changed my life
No matter how much it has hurt me
No matter how hard I have loved
We were all made for each other
or else you wouldn't have found us

I believe in you, because I want to
Because it makes sense to me
and it feels right

It still blows my mind how reminding you
Just how special you are
Makes me feel so special

Setbacks
You're missing when I need you the most
I cut you up with brutal words
You don't even flinch
I guess you always knew I'd forgive you

What does this make of me
who does this make me out to be
And the things they say
I already fight your battles
I have been defending you
and I still plan to

My heart is hurting, a little less everyday
because now when I reach out to you
I don't see you reaching away
Instead I hear your words echoing
In the back of my mind like they always have
I guess I'll always want you back

The irony, it destroys me
Nothing about you has ever been mine
but when I'm lost and hurt and broken
it's your strength that I rely on every time

Sometimes when we're driving down a crowded street
I am convinced the whole world is staring at me
Wondering how I got you
And I don't even mind that they look at you amazed
Because I am too
and you, you're everything
Everything I could have hoped for you
Surpassing all my dreams
and then, there's the way you handle me
Despite my rough reactions
You respond so delicately
We both know I'm a train wreck
An accident waiting to happen
But there's something else you see in me
When I don't know why you stand me

It must be tough being you
On our bad days
Granted
You usually cause them
But the hate that I resort to
In order to hurt you back
The awful things I say
Knowing you already believe them
The awful threats I make
Knowing it would kill you to see them
The jabs I throw
I shoot really, really low

Guilt follows
I'm supposed to be your safe place
And instead
I bring you pain

And this is how it continues
We mend
We fall back in love
And then you get spooked by the calm
You throw a tiny match
To my gasoline shield
And then I am determined
To make everything burn

But the difference is
I ache
Knowing that I hurt you
It haunts me
And you
There's just as much pain that you deliver
But you only remember
What you receive

Monday night
I blew out candles
And I used my wish on you
On your health
On your safety
On your sanity
I wished for you
I wished for us
I wished for better

And then
I felt the wind knocked out of me
Because once again it occurred to me
I'd give up every important thing
I'd sacrifice everything of my own
For you to be happy

There's just you now
I no longer exist
I chased myself away

Some of the bravest
Most brilliant souls I have known
Were also somehow
The weakest
And most afraid
And I don't know how
But I loved each of them
Passionately
Willingly
Because I saw their struggle
I saw that they too were confused
With how many different versions of themselves
They were forced to live as
Moment to moment

And on the days they disappointed me
I knew that their disappointment in themselves
Would hurt them more than it could ever hurt me
But on the days they made me proud
Man, I knew for sure
That they were on top of the world

And you see
Sometimes
It's so humbling to love someone
Who is so weak and so scared
It's so easy to write off the disappointment
Because a good day
Meant the most precious soul in my world
Saw me as the most prized in theirs

Loving you wasn't a challenge
I did that effortlessly
It was dealing with your many sides
That took the life out of me
On edge constantly
Not knowing which person was coming out next
Caused me to create new sides of myself
And decide by the moment
Which version you would get
So much time has passed
That I no longer know who's who
Who's evil, who's good
I used to be sure that I was the victim
But now I love you like a monster would
Nothing is about easing your pain
It's only about making you feel what I do
And the only way to stay on your level
Is to fight off your love with abuse
Abuse I learned from you

My heart is fine
The pain is in my ego
The idea that I wasn't good enough
Patient enough
Loving enough
The idea that your inability
To be a compassionate, functioning human
Is at all a reflection of me
And what I brought to the relationship
That's where it hurts
In the unknown
The fact that somehow
I'm able to blame myself
For you not wanting to be a better person

And it lingers
A heavy weight in my spirit
Knowing that I would have done anything
To save you
But it hurts even more to accept
That you're too afraid to be saved

I have a scar on my left leg
A cut from your twin bed
The one we shared for months
When you were at your lowest
And every time I see that scar
It sends me such mixed emotions
I remember how pure we were
How nothing mattered but us
But then the reality occurs to me
Loving you left me with a scar
No matter how far I run
How much I move on
You left a mark
Proof that I'll always carry these memories
Proof that I'll always be tied to you

You have behaved like such a monster
I no longer see you as a person
The things I know about your past
I mix them with hate and use them against you
Because I don't believe you actually feel a thing
I swear they're just defense mechanisms
Ways to keep me in the fight
But every now and then I wonder
What if
What if you're not all monster
What if you really did love me
What if all the evil I use against you
Really does pain you

But the way you approach me
There's just no way to know

Making pizza with you at 3am
Sharing Doritos while it bakes
Laughing about the last episode of New Girl
Your hands holding my face
It feels like it's lifetimes and lifetimes away
And yet it feels brand new
It's like no matter how awful we get
I hold onto the good in you
And though these precious memories
Get further and further away
with the first pang of loneliness
I start to see them as yesterday
And the past 8 months of torture
Start to dissipate
As I create kindness out of miscommunication
And lie your evil away

Which would I rather lose
My creativity or my sanity?

That's the struggle I face
When it comes to letting you go

I can get my mind
And my soul back
Just by moving on

But letting go
And losing you
Means
Giving up my muse

I remember when we first met

I was so excited to learn

How many important dates we had in common

So many significant people in our lives

Sharing birthdays and parallel adventures

As if the universe had left little breadcrumbs

So that when we found each other

We'd know for sure

And we did

But it didn't go the way we planned

So now there's all these important dates

Attached to all my significant people

And forever haunted by you

I know I have to relive pieces of us
In order to heal
And I'm nervous to graze back over the pain
To run my fingers over the bruised places
And remember how it felt to be betrayed
To be promised overwhelming love
But met with lies and manipulations
I know that will be difficult
But I know that I can bear it

It's the happy I'm afraid to revisit
The Sunday mornings that turn into Sunday nights
When we realize we never left the bed
The early morning texts when we slept apart
The look in your eyes when I surprised you
By bringing your favorite snack
Even more so when a love note was attached
I'm terrified to re-hear the lyrics
That we used to scribble onto notepads
Afraid to relive the night that you carved
Our names into the coffee table
It's the good that haunts me

And it's painful knowing
That in order to recover
I have to wash out all of the good
And focus on the bad
Remind myself every day what I left
So that I never fantasize
About going back
So I have to ride this rollercoaster
Flipping back and forth
Ricocheting between
"I'll never love like this again"
And "I don't love you anymore"

I wish I could make you understand our tie
How when you're hurting yourself
Or doing something that you know would hurt me
I can feel it

My chest tightens up
Gloom hangs over me
I can feel the world closing in

But when you're clean
When your spirit and your heart are free
I can feel the relief in my bones
I can feel how much you mean to me

Sometimes I wonder if you could grasp
How tightly we are wound together
If it would make you think twice before jumping off the ledge
But then I worry that maybe if you knew for sure
How much pain you really cause me
That it would only make you want to hurt me more

I can feel myself caring

Less and less as the days go on

I used to panic that you were slipping away

Now I'm consciously pushing you

But then I snap

The idea of there being anyone else

Even though I don't want you to be mine

My ego isn't ready for the blow

Isolation is a tactic

Be very wary of feeling lonely

When you're next to the person you "love"

Toxic people will pull you from your comfort zone

And push you into danger

All while disguising it as a testament of love

It'll be much, much too late

Before you realize the newfound distance

You accidentally put between you and your lifelines

And as their toxicity spreads

And you become more and more infected

They'll remind you that you are all alone

And can rely on only them

All while stripping away any bit of security

And proving themselves anything but reliable

If you feel lonely,

It isn't love

I think more about my mistakes than yours
Things I said out of anger
Reactions you pushed me to
Lies I had to tell to get your attention
Sleepless nights fueled by abuse
Every time I try to be honest with myself
And relive those moments as they truly were
I almost feel as if I'm not taking responsibility
As if I'm passing all the blame
And that's what halts the healing the most
Being the victim of love gone horrific
And yet, feeling so much shame

My favorite thing about love stories
And tragedies
And everything in between
Is the friendships

The people who stood by
Putting ice on your wounds
Patiently listening
While everything they warned of
Is slowly revealed to be reality
The friends who continue to cheer on
Despite setbacks and resistance
And always, always pushed
For hearts to be followed
Those are the heroes in the stories
The supporting characters
The tribe

I thank the universe every day for mine

So many conversations I'm able to recall
Of you telling me over and over again
That I deserve nothing at all
Nights I laid in bed in tears
Hoping I'd do something right
Something amazing
Something to get your attention
And change your mind
Inspire you to validate me
But you won't

And now I sit here thinking
About how soon I'll see my own words in print
I'll take all this pain you forced on me
And I'll make something of it
And I'll be poised
And I'll use grace
But no matter how much recognition
No matter how much praise
There will always be an empty hole in me
Knowing I could never please you

For a while I let that truth silence me
Living in fear of my own success
Knowing it would just give you
More things to take credit for
As if I'm handing you a well-lit platform
To rip me down from
But the reality of it is
I'm choosing not to hide
Whether it be behind closed doors
Or in front of the world
in spite of you,
I'll thrive

I've made a lot of wishes
Since I found you
I wished for more time
More life with you
I wished for your healing
For you to find strength
For you to find hope
I wished for patience
So that I could love you better
I wished I could take your pain away
That I could love it out of you
I wished that I could show you
How good life could be
If you would let it
I wished and I wished
Always for you
So there could be us
And now that we're done
The hardest thing to let go of
Is my faith in you
Most days I want to believe
You have it in you to change
But I know that if I don't find a way
To accept the reality of you
I'll spend my life alone
Making wishes

Torn, in love
Unable to feel whole
Strains on my heart
Damage to my soul

Searching for truth
But there is no truth to find
For I know not what answer I seek
My heart vs. my mind

The abuse is apparent
No energy to hurt anymore
We have struggled for peace
Yet we are constantly at war

Feelings on edge
The anxiety reaches a peak
The rage fills me with desires
Monsters I dare not feed
But my demons never starve
They feast when you're in need
And what I cannot devour
You use to starve me

And so I wonder every day
And again later as I struggle with sleep
Is the problem that you're barely here
Or that you're always with me

Now we're at the point that I keep my distance
I hide my feelings for you
I cry on my own time
I avoid vulnerability at all costs
I love you in ways I'm dying to explain
But I just can't stand them knowing

Eyes open wide in the dark of the night
It's feeling like revenge
All the words you've ever spoken are broken now
When enemies started off as friends
I hope you soaked up every tear I shared
Because you'll never see them again

Trust, it breaks, it fades away
I'll leave it in the past, with our friendship

Oh it's going to taste so, so sweet
Just like you did that first night
That you told the world you loved me
And I gave in because I believed
We could be better
Better if we were together

I guess the times have changed
Along with our clouded minds
And to think,
I used to love you all the time
But I'm feeling judgmental tonight

I made my moves too soon
Totally underestimated you and your mood
It all rests heavy in the back of my mind
But I just can't afford to lose sleep

While we were dancing
I lost my will
I should have kept my eyes open
And my knees still
But instead I let you lead
I guess the joke is on me

You can hold my hand at the very end
And we can forget this ever happened
But first, you're gonna make it up to me

And oh, it's going to taste so, so sweet
It's a dangerous game
When the blood flows in the form of words
We all drink to regret
But there's no way my heart can forget
The night I found enemies in friends

I love you with so much confusion
It changes day to day
And sometimes I can't help
But realize the turmoil you must face
Knowing that at any moment
I might love it away

Forever
We used to say that
Now I wonder if I ever believed
If I ever truly thought it was possible
Was I ever even happy?
I glance over our story
And I realize the fondness is gone
I don't see you with love
I only see the monster
I only feel the pain
And the thing that makes these revelations so strange
Is where I place the blame
Instead of holding it against you
For the torment and the abuse
I am angry at myself
Forever creating sweetness in you
For setting the bar so incredibly low
That I imagined you jumping through hoops
For loving myself so very little
That I accepted so little from you

It has come to this
We've traveled the sun so many times
Broken up and reconciled
I'm back at the beginning again
Revisiting the maybes
Maybe this time will be different
Maybe we won't bring up the past
Maybe we're not angry anymore

Maybe I don't want to be happy

Toxic relationship guilt
I'm carrying a lot of it
In really unreliable bags
The weird thing is
It's not about my actual relationship
It's about all the people along the way
That suffered at the hands
Of my bad relationship choices
Those who heard the screaming and the name calling
Those who noticed the bruises and the scrapes

Those that were pulled into your charm
Thinking they met the man of their dreams
Only to have that rug pulled out by me
People who were promised the world
Only to realize you still owed me so much more
I crossed the paths of so many people
I never, ever would have encountered
If I wasn't tracing the footsteps of a damaged man

And I'm sorry
To every single soul that was touched negatively
While I sorted through the mess
I'm sorry for dragging you under with me
Sorry for acting on emotion
Sorry for being so confident
Sorry for not showing you my best

Triggers are like fishing bait
They're tied to our past
And dipped into our present
Just praying they'll get a bite
Hoping we'll latch on
Provoked, committed to the pain
The holder of the line has one goal
Inspire us to fight back to fiercely
That we walk blindly into our own demise
Our triggers, our bad memories
They're not what does us in It's our reaction to them
Our inability to process the pain
And truly let it go

On the days I love you
I watch you adoringly
Me on my knees
You on the pedestal I imagined for you
Nothing compares

On the days I hate you
I look back at you in disgust
You crawling through the filth you choose
Me watching from my high horse
How can we be both?

How is it
That you are
The greatest person I've ever known
And yet the biggest disappointment
I've ever felt

And even more complicated is
I know for sure
You see me the same way
And so we struggle
Not at all good enough for each other
And still too good to take the time

I'm not feeling lonely, just insecure

If I was lonely

I'd be finding ways to see you

Instead

I'm just finding ways to get noticed

My only crime is trying to love you
And now I'll serve a life sentence
Stricken by pain and confusion
Finding wreckage everywhere
Even where the calm may be
I can't reside in normalcy
Because I loved you
I committed myself to chaos
And here I'll live
For the rest of my life
Being punished every day
Because you were weak

I'd take your fists over your words any day
Never thought I'd miss a time
Where I'd watch bruises fade away
And I'd feel strong knowing I could get through
Bruises, they're nothing compared to
The damage that your words do
I would bleed weakness and I would grow tall
Brave enough to raise a hand
Bold enough to deny fault
Attempt to even the score and feed into your sick games
Desperate for the world to see my growth
I'd secretly hope the wounds would stay
Instead I got more than I bargained for
These scars beneath the skin
No one can see them but they're becoming evident
To all the people I don't let in
They praise and watch me with eyes glowing softly
Whispering words anyone would do backflips to hear
Instead I hate them for trying to manipulate me
Completely condemned by disgust and fear
I hope you know you did this to me
With your claims of unconditional love
The ones that proceeded harmful blows and were followed by violent shoves
And all the terrible things you told me about me
Well I guess maybe I do believe
And no matter what I work towards
I am always going to be
That little girl that wasn't good enough
The kid you didn't have to keep
The package that you inherited
In a deal you didn't really need
Most days I want to thank you
For making me such a tough case to crack
But instead I'm bitter and broken
Unable to love anyone back
And they probably really do like me
They can't all tell lies that well
And maybe, just maybe I'm not that shitty
But when I hear you talk about me...
I'd never be able to tell

You used your love like a weapon
Smothering me with it
And then ripping it away
Leaving me in a constant state of anxiety
Never knowing what feelings were safe

Every time I felt happiness
I was on edge knowing that
At any moment it could disappear
Walking on your strategically placed eggshells
Living our love story in fear

But when I was tossed aside
Defeated and aching
I clung to the hope that you built for me
Knowing that at any moment
You could come back
And shower me with love and apologies

And that's how I got caught in the trap
For more time than I care to say
Riding someone's emotional rollercoaster
Waiting around to be loved
And accepting it in absolutely any shape

You spent years chipping away at me

And I thought I would slowly dissolve

You'd peel back so much that I'd have nothing left

And I'd no longer exist

But instead, you acted as an ice pick

Removing all my unneeded baggage

Releasing me from the blurry mess

Revealing who I was always meant to be

Your goal was always to erase

But instead you set me free

I realized that if I write it down
In my own words
I take its power away

All the anger
The abuse
The manipulation
The control

It consumed me
Dictated my every mood
Every emotion

But now that I can read it back
See my story from beginning to end
Follow every lie
Every ache
Every abrupt change
I know for sure that only I can decide
How I'm willing to be treated
And how I choose to respond
To those who just want to test me

I honestly don't know what's worse

Spending years begging for love
From someone who isn't capable
Draining every resource
Every depth
Or realizing through your recovery from them that
You never truly loved them anyway
And you weren't seeking to ease their pain
You were hoping to conceal your own

In moments of silence I realize I battle more with my ego
than my heart
My feelings aren't hurt that the love may be gone
My spirit is struggling with the idea that it was never there

I feel awful saying it but
This is the one time that I enjoy
Watching history repeat itself
Everything you told her
Every truth you twisted
Alarms go off in my head
Of our first few months
And it knocks the wind out of me
But each time it hits me
It takes less and less time to find my breath
And I know it's only a matter of time
Before it doesn't hit me at all

I knew by the way you kissed me goodbye
That the thrill was finally gone
I watched you walk to your car
My soul draining from me
It's so painful to know that we don't want this anymore
And even more painful to know that we'll keep fighting
for it anyway

I just want you to know
That when it's all said and done
When the night finally comes
And our war is silenced
And you're alone trying to sort through
What's left of the feelings you haven't numbed
I'm there with you
Right next to you
Loving you anyway
And I know you can't feel me anymore
I know you've numbed me out too
But I'm always right there
Holding on
Hoping to appeal to you
Hoping you'll choose to save yourself

Only time will tell
Or at least that's what they say
But the only thing time has been telling me
Is that the confusion never goes away

So I wait and wait for answers
And of course, they never show
Oh how I wish I could accept that non-action is an
answer
Then maybe I could let you go

Every day I am thankful

That you'll never understand

Never comprehend

The loneliness and the weight

That comes along with calling a phone

Over and over and over again

How damaging it is

To sit outside the bathroom door

Not knowing if I should be banging

Not knowing if I'll have to kick it down

The anger that accompanies

The relentless begging

And the sorrow and defeat that follows

Not being heard

I'm so glad you'll never know how painful it is

To call hospitals and describe the person you love

Praying that someone will say

"Yes, he's here, but that is all we can say"

I'm so glad that you'll never suffer that way

Never suffer the way I have from loving you

You were never wrong to love someone

No matter what they put you through
No matter how crazy you felt
No matter the same, the guilt, the upset
You were never wrong to give someone a chance

The fault is theirs for missing the opportunity

Your love is still strong enough to heal
They just weren't done being broken

In the big scheme of things
It doesn't matter if you love me or not
Because you treat me like I don't mater
Therefore, I don't matter

But so badly I wish I could dig in there
I just know in my heart
I'd find the smallest bit of devotion

Reserved for us, meant for me
And I don't know why it matters
But it matters

I release you to the universe
I used to dream of this day
Setting you free into the world
Clean, saved, fixed
But in the dream, you never wandered
You were free as a bird
Yet planted next to me

Instead
I'm releasing you today
Conniving, damaged, unwilling
And I don't know if you'll decide to wander
But I'm no longer carrying you along for the ride
You have to find soul on your own
You're no longer chained to mine

Actual flutters in my heart
I lose my breath
And when I gasp for air
I see your face
And it's like I can feel you gasping too

And when I'm tingly and can't sleep
I awake to pains shooting through my shins
I know you're out there somewhere
Kicking restless legs

And when my soul aches
Just longing to be closer to yours
It's as if I feel it leaving my body
It only gets so far before returning
And I truly believe it's because
It found and bounced off yours

Sometimes I wish we weren't soulmates
Because I struggle every day
Just trying to feel my own feelings
And it's so, so heavy to have to feel yours too

If you were to ask why I stay
Id' have to let you know
I'm more afraid of meeting a monster I am not accustomed to
Then I am of letting the familiar one go

Every day is a blur
I don't know whose side
I am on
Yours or mine

Sometimes I'm beating down the enemy
Sometimes I'm fighting for my life

I hope you remember fondly
Remember the me that loved you

Don't remember me as I was on
On a snowed in Wednesday
After 10 hours of being passive with each other
Crowded on the couch
Watching cartoons on your iPad
While you hide behind your phone
Trying to up my anxiety
Trying to push my buttons
I swear you watch my blood rise

Don't remember me on a bad day
Remember me on Thursday morning
When I came back to bring you donuts
With cute notes on the box
Remember me on Sunday afternoon
After we've been buried in each other
Since the night before

Reminisce of me kindly

And now I realize what I am asking of you
And what I'm thankful you haven't asked of me

What I mean to say is
Let me go and live your life
It's best not to remember me

And when love finally came around

I almost didn't notice it

Because as it turns out

I had no idea what it looked like

I loved you so hard
I ruined you for all future love
No one will ever see you
Get you, understand you
Know you, please you
Infuriate you
No one will ever love you like I did
But you'll spend the rest of your life looking for it
Believing it's easy to find
Because you found it once before
In me

And you
You ruined me for all future love
But not because you loved me too good
Because you belittled me and shamed me
Made me believe I was crazy
Convinced me that I couldn't possibly be loved
Not even by you
You were settling for me out of the kindness of your heart
And I'd be a fool to let you get away
And I will spend the rest of my life
Wanting nothing more than to learn
What love actually feels like
And yet I'll subconsciously avoid it all costs
Because anyone who gives me attention
Might "love" the way that you do
And try to ruin me too

You're out there
Somewhere
And she's next to you
Wearing that ring
And me I'm over here
Alone on purpose
Pretending not to feel a thing

And I'm not angry at you
For choosing someone else
Or for letting someone else choose you
I'm just a little hurt
Or maybe more disturbed
That I know you still think of me too

Sometimes
I regret every choosing freedom
I regret ever saying no
But I think that maybe a part of me
Truly believed
You'd never really go

And it's not that I feel like I lost
It's just that I feel as if
The loss might be mine
And it's painful, you know
To have to relive our time together
And remember I traded you in
For pride

It's not you that I want to leave behind
If it was up to me
I'd be taking you with me
But the version of myself that I become
When we're at war
I despise her
And I don't want to be associated with her anymore
But getting rid of her means losing you
And it's not an easy decision
And I'm sure I'll fuck up again soon
But I really, really, really need to try
To love myself more than I love you

I wish I could love you straight
I wish you could show me more compassion
More patience
More understanding
I wish loving you unconditionally
Would inspire you to heal
But instead
It just feeds your assumption that I'm weak
You do wrong and I love you through it
I must be weak
I must be insane
And you just can't get your shit together
To waste your life with an insane person
The cycle

I knew early on you weren't the one for me

But I so badly wanted to be the one for you

I knew you needed saving

Hope

Desire

Someone to get consumed by

And I so badly wanted to be your one

That I forgot I'd be sacrificing my own

It has never been this dark
Or if it has, I don't remember
Even when I'm awake and alert
I move as if my eyes are closed
Slowly
My arms outstretched
So I don't disturb anyone
So I don't cause any injury
I feel so fragile
But in the way of a ticking time bomb
And I know that at any moment
I could explode
And ruin everything in my wake
But the person that used to live inside of me
Knows how much everything around me means to me
And is pleading with me, constantly
"Don't detonate
Hold out just a little bit longer
You can pull through this
And everyone can survive it"
I hear you, self
And I believe

But it's just so fuckin dark in here

As we've suffered more
Endured more
Inflicted more
I realize I'm not as much worried with you forgiving me
I don't need to make amends
There's no need for me
To apologize for the abuse I turned to
In order to defend myself
Against my abuser
What I need to focus on
Is forgiving myself
For lowering my standards
For ignoring the signs
For believing you could change
For loving you anyway
For acting out of rage
For seeking closure
For being weak
And then for being strong enough to walk away

I need to forgive myself
Before I feel anything else
And the funny thing is
That through making peace with myself
I know
That I'll forgive you too
And I guess that's just a bonus

You throw my insecurities at me
Like you're tossing razor blades at a target
It doesn't matter where they land
As long as they Knick me just a little bit
Enough to inspire a small bleed
Just the tiniest of scars
That no amount of love and care can fade
Just a little something for me to keep forever
A sign that you were once here
And proved that I was weak

I watched you sleep

My heart racing

Caressed your face

You pulled me in tighter

Exhaled deeply

As if you finally felt safe

And for the first time

In a long time

So did I

But the sun always rises

And the phone always rings

And the world always disrupts us

If only we lived on a planet

Of just you and me

Then maybe we could be happy in love

I have given my soul
In an attempt to save yours

And now we're both fucked

And to make things worse
We can't even figure out a way to stay together
So not only are we fucked
But so are the lonely souls we attach ourselves to next

And so it goes
How one by one everybody loses their mind
All in an attempt
To be loved

Dancing across the kitchen floor

Absolutely melting to your laugh

I forget there was a world outside of us

And that's when I should have known it would never

work

The exact second that I decided there was only us

Because it was then that

I took away the importance of me

I truly believe that you love me
Though statistics say
You just aren't capable
I believe the thought of life without me
Brings you worry
Because I think you look at me as a prize
And if you can keep
Someone like me
Then maybe you aren't so bad
But then again
Maybe you don't love me
As much as you envy me
I'm such a consistent supply

There are times I am sure
We were made with each other in mind
You predict my every move
And I'm more than happy to be understood by you
It's as if no matter what the universe throws
We stay on the exact same page
I live happily for those days

Then there are times I am sure
We have exhausted our connection
No matter what I say or do
I can't seem to get through to you
And your responses seem like a different language
I just can't figure you out
Or relate to you in anyway
I live in dread of those days

I rehearse final lines
Convinced we can't continue this way
I take deep breaths, I'm prepared for pain
And then you greet me with a different day
You predict that I'm at my wits end
Plead that you can't bear to lose me again
Our hearts align in a way that makes me ache
There's nothing quite like being understood

No one has challenged you
The way that I do
And I think it makes you
Love and hate me
In equal measure
And your struggle isn't
Whether you need me or not
It's if having me on your arm
Makes you feel accomplished
Or makes you feel inferior
And that changes a little bit
Each day

I can't even stomach
The things I have said to you
In attempts to push you away
It only reminds me
How hurtful I can be
Reminds me that I'm ashamed
And then I remember
The awful things you said to me
That inspired me to push back
And that's how the cycle goes
Remorse
Regret
Anger
Repeat

There are absolutely no excuses

For what you have put me through

But if you sit tight

I'm sure I can make some up for you

How dare you
Push me away
So violently
And then throw a tantrum
When I stay gone

You can't have it both ways
And you certainly can't
Pick and choose
Which pieces of me
Are worth keeping

I love so hard and so deep
That I will hold on
And fight for something
Far longer than I should
But eventually
I will let go
And when I do
It will be as if you never existed
I let go with such force
That you'll never be able to

Latch back on

Love me less
Less than you have
Less than you do

Love me more
Show me something

Let me go
I'm tired of being held on to

Cling to me
I can't stand to be released

Answer me
Tell me something
I need to hear

Ignore my pleas
Don't even try to humor me

Come closer
I can't stand that you're away

Keep your distance
You terrify me

The worse evil
I'll never know it

It's not that I don't want to love you anymore
I'd just like to love you less than I love myself
But I worry that I'm in too deep now
I'll never get my worth back

I wish I could get to know you
Without your mask
Without your walls

I wish there was more to you
Wish you knew how to dig deep
So badly I want you to
Be able to feel the way I love you

I wonder too often
What caused it
Why you hurt so bad
And why you prefer it so much

That's why I used to watch you sleep
I thought maybe
I could pull something real out of you
If I kissed you
While you were at peace

I just wish there was more to us
More than passion and flames
How can you love someone so deeply
And still not feel a thing

I'm exhausted
It has become easier for me
To fake my way
Through every day
It's a shame
I shut off my feelings
To everything good
So that I can feel your pain

I don't know how
You can miss someone
Who sucks the very life out of you
But sometimes I do

Maybe
I'm addicted to being drained

Nothing terrifies me
Or thrills me more
Than kissing you
Either it's our last kiss
And it's just perfect enough
To force a goodbye
Or it'll be like every other perfect kiss
That we swore was our last
And end up
Being just another beginning

You should
Worship the ground
I fuckin walk on

Not because
I paid your way
Or dried your tears
Not because I kept you alive
Or fought for you
Not because I defended you
And had your back
When no one else did
Not because I loved you
Nonstop
When you were so fuckin unlovable
You should just worship
The ground I walk on
Because I am the woman
You claim to love

Everything else
Should have just been reminders
To stay in line

When we first met
You told your aunt
That you had found your soulmate
And that you just knew
Your whole life
Was about to get better

And then you proceeded to use me
And beat me down
For over a year
And I allowed you to
Because I kept going back
To that one thing
Your aunt told me

Imagine
Holding onto something
So fuckin terrible
Because they said
One nice thing to someone else

Imagine
Enduring endless abuse
Holding out
For one false promise

Imagine
Finding your soulmate
And completely destroying them

I'm slowly feeling the weight
Roll off my shoulders
It's like I'm being reborn

And I might not maintain
I could slip up
And let you in again
...and that's okay

But one day
I'll be brave enough
To push all the way through
And I really will be

Reborn

Sometimes
Even when you know
That you're being abused
And you know
That things can't get better
There's still that
Tiny human part of you
That sees the good
In your abuser
And it becomes hard to believe
That one person
Could hold so much evil
While having so much charm
And that's what keeps the cycle alive
A driving need to see
How long you can stretch out
The little bit of good

Thanks for all the lies
I'll keep them forever
In forms of twisted beliefs
I'll recall them always
Every time someone misspeaks
Or forgets a detail
I'll think of you
My monster
And forever I'll worry
That you have come for me
In the likeness of a new man
From now on
Everyone might as well be a monster
Because I'm surely
Going to see them as one

I feel so grateful
That our story will live on forever
In these pages
Even if it presents in darkness
We'll always know what is was

And I feel so pleased -
Smug even
That our story will live on forever
In these pages
Because it presents the truth
And I'll always know who you are

I am an addict
And my narcissist is my drug
More
And more
And more
I need it
And then I get it
And while I'm feeling the effects
Swimming in highs
Being smothered with lows
The whole time
I'm thinking about how much I hate this
How I hate being an addict
And hate having a drug

But then I hit that lull
And I just need to feel something
Or I'm feeling too much
And I just want to be numb
Whatever the push may be
The truth remains
And haunts me
I am an addict
and you are my drug

I want you to come complete

◇◇◇◇◇◇◇◇

"I really thought I'd be the one to make you change"

And there it is
All my mistakes summed up
I came into it knowing you weren't whole

Loving you
Is like drinking labeled poison
I know
That it's eventually going to kill me
But I just can't help it
This deep buried urge
To keep on drinking
Just to see how much I can take

Just to experience that moment
At the very end
Where I know I have ingested
That final drop
Just to feel the life being sucked out of me
What a release
And the only way I can escape you

Loving a narcissist
Changes the way you see
And interact with the world

Compliments become lifelines
A stranger's kindness
Is suddenly what keeps you moving forward
Because the person you love
Has you convinced
That You only deserve heartache

Affection becomes skeptical
Nothing feels genuine
Because you have learned
That even the softest of touches
Has a motive

Every word spoken is a riddle
No matter how simple the sentence
You will dissect it
Until you find the loophole
Until you spot the lie
Because there's no more
Reliable words

Every missed phone call
Now becomes strategic
And you just know whoever
Was meant to be on the other end
Is avoiding you
Because you have learned
That you deserve to be punished
And sometimes the worst punishment
Is delivered through silence

Insults roll right off your shoulder
Yet settle themselves deep in your soul
And your boundaries disappear
The person you love the most
Has already made you out to be the worst
So nothing that anyone says
Really sinks in
You know who are now
Because you've been told

And the strangest thing
About loving a narcissist
Is that sometimes you know
You remind yourself every morning
That the problem isn't you
That they're sick and they're damaged
That you're the sane one
The strong one
The one better off
You tell yourself over and over again
That they have got you all wrong
And that you can get yourself back
You can heal and you can beat them

But then those voices start chattering
And those nerves start kicking in
And you think that maybe
Just maybe
You can heal you both of you
If you put yourself on the back burner
For just a little longer
And love the narcissist

I remember the first time you took me home
Your family didn't even look my way
I should've taken it as a sign
They were used to girls coming and going quickly

You made a joke about your mom being excited
Because she thought I was your ex
I should've known right then
The false competition you'd create

You tossed the football around with your cousin
Everything came so naturally
I was hooked on your confidence
And questioning my own

It's strange to look back
Knowing what I know now
I was intrigued at how tough you seemed
And by now I've watched you crumble

Is it love or pity?
Do I worry that you'll fall apart without me?
Or do I worry that you'll flourish?
I don't know which would hurt more

Is it love ...or codependence
Do I worry that I'll fall apart without you?
Or do I worry that I'll flourish?
I don't know which would hurt more

◇◇◇◇◇◇◇

Maybe if I convince myself that I hate you
I can end the agony
But I don't know where the cord lies
Am I tied to believing I love you
Or hooked on thinking you love me

This isn't romantic anymore
I had made such a fairy tale out of you
Out of us
I knew the stories
I knew the likelihood
I knew risk
But I believed anyway

I remember so many nights
Sitting in front of you
My soul aching
Crying, begging, pleading
Asking for explanations
Expecting an emotion
Needing validation
You'd meet me with blank stares
"I don't know what to tell you"
Proceeds the shrugs of your weak shoulders
I hate you so much
But I need to hear that I earned this pain
I need you to admit what you've done
I need to hear the truth

So that I can cope with my next move
But it never comes
Just conversations going in circles
Until you manage to turn it on me
And before I know it I'm replaying my own behavior
Dissecting my own responses
Feeling fuckin guilty
How dare I kick a man who's already down

I wake abruptly at 3am realizing that I have been duped again
You're lying next to me, sound asleep
Not a thing could shake you
I feel the courage build in me
Feel myself getting strong
Pack my shit and do what I should've done all along
Your groggy arms reach for me
"Oh, leaving again ...and in the middle of the night..?"
And those words go right through me
"Who's the coward now" I think to myself
It's me
The dumb bitch crawling back into bed

It doesn't matter
It just doesn't matter
I repeat it over and over to myself
Every time I want to text
Every time I want to call
"I just want to end it on a good note"
I try and convince myself
But I know if you answer
That it will come to blows
And I know that if you don't
I'll keep calling and calling and calling

There's no closure with a narcissist
It's part of their game
No explanations
No validation
No steady goodbye
You'll always be waiting for an apology
Always be waiting for sense to be made
And the truth is
It doesn't matter
It just doesn't matter

You have to come up for air

Loving an addict is like living underwater
You can still get around
But it goes in slow motion
And takes all your energy
The breaths you can manage are painful
Your eyes burn
No one can hear your screams
And it truly feels like
You'll never reach the top
No matter how hard you kick
How quickly you move your arms
How strongly you believe
You just can't quite escape
And the truth is
It doesn't even matter if you break the surface
Because as soon as you see the light
You'll feel the tug at your ankle
And you'll be sucked back under

It always humbles
And saddens me
To see people's surprise
When they hear my story
When they hear that
I let half a human suck me dry
That I allowed
An insecure man
To reach his dirty hands
Inside my soul
And try to take the good parts out
They look at me confused
Compliment me on my strength
"I never could have imagined...
That would happen to you"

So I wonder
What do the abused look like
The sad
The beaten down
The broken
Those barely hanging on
How do we see them coming
Because if I'm the poster
For able and strong
I'm so worried about the others

Because I'm the abused
The sad
The broken
Some days
I'm just barely hanging on

"There's no place like home"
Holds a different meaning for me
Everywhere feels safer than home
When you're living with a monster

Every phone call
Is a bad one
Every hang out
Is a sad one
Every time you kiss me
You take another piece of me
Yet if you say you won't see me
You awaken the beast in me

I can't fuckin stand you
When you're lying next to me
Fast asleep
While I agonize and stress
Trying to figure out how
I got here again
Why
I let you win

The morning comes
And you're on my nerves
I text my best friend
About how you drain my soul I
"It's definitely over this time
He's just not the one"
I'm so sure of it too

Until you lie and say you're done
How dare you beat me to it
Now I need to win you back

How can you dislike something so much
And yet sacrifice your sanity to keep it
How does someone cause you so much fuckin pain
And you beg them to let you feel it

Tonight's the night
You're on your way
And I know for sure
I'm going to tell you it's over
And I'm going to mean it
Though you won't believe it
Until I play it so Coolly
That you begin to unnerve
So you flip the script

And hide your hurt
Instead you spew insults
To get me to react
And even though I don't even want you
Now I have to get you back

"You look sad"
It hits harder than most words
It's noticeable now
Everyone can see it
The life has been sucked out of me
And now everyone knows that I've changed
I laugh it off
"I'm sooo tired"
I rebuttal
But everyone knows
Tired and sad just aren't the same

My mom asked how I was last week
And I told her I felt like an empty shell
As if every human trait inside of me
Had been completely removed
Just an empty shell
Going through the motions
You've won again

And I'm just tired

In me

You met your match

Light a fire under me

And I'll light one right back

Whatever move you make

I'm one step ahead

By the time your knife reaches me

You're bleeding to death

You may conquer

Every now and then

You might be successful

At sucking me in

But do not be fooled

By my occasional weakness

My foundation does not shake

You may be able

To twist , bend and beat me

But you'll be the one to break

I keep remembering all the bad shit
To remind me to stay away from you
But all the bad shit
Just reminds me that I tolerated you
And then I feel shitty about me
And all that I've contributed, too
And it's a vicious cycle
One I seem to cling on to
I worry all the time that I'll never get better

I want to apologize
I want to end things civilly
Both of us accepting with kindness
That were just not meant to be
But we try and smooth things over
And then you take a jab at me
Next thing I know, insults are flying
And you get me, right where you want me

Love
I want to believe it's all about love
About hope and fate
About promise and change
I want to believe that we keep testing each other
And that one day we'll wake up sure

We'll know that we've beat the odds
And we don't have to punish each other anymore
I wait and wait and wait for the day
But punish myself every day in between

It's more ego than it is hurt
God forbid you move on and do better
Not better than me, but do better than you've done
For me
Be better to them then you've been towards me
I think of all the times
You couldn't just let us be happy
And any time I was close to loving you openly
You'd find a way to torture me
And there's a level of crazy that exists
And that's where you need to keep me
In order to keep me
I ache over how different it could be

And it will be different
When I learn to accept
That I'm better off without you
No matter how much I love you
I'm better off without you

The scariest thing about us
Is that we got to a place
Where no boundaries existed
There was nothing you could do
That would make me say when
I just kept holding on
Kept enduring
Kept believing
Kept waiting for the moment
That changed it all
I just knew you'd get it together
And give me the love I deserved
And then you didn't
Again and
Again and
Again

Here's to saying when

Tonight
I can't stop crying
We've been at this for 20 months
We've ended it a million times
We've exchanged ugly words
Hands have been thrown
We've broken each other's hearts
Time and time again
And woke up the next day
Like nothing ever happened
Reconciled
As if destroying each other was okay
But tonight
It's as if reality has set in

I can't live like this anymore
Waiting for you to decide
Whether you're going to love me properly or not
Waiting for you to decide
Whether you're going to be a better person or not
Waiting for you to decide
What I'm worth
Maybe I have finally realized
That I have all the power
To decide how I should feel

And for tonight
I have decided to cry it out

insomnia

◇◇◇◇◇◇◇◇◇

Wide awake

A thousand thoughts rushing my brain
I force my eyes closed
I beg for sleep
And not because I need it
Just because I need this day to be over

You're the only one

Who makes me feel butterflies
After so many years
My nerves still kick in
My stomach turns
My hands shake
You look me over
And I feel my heart race
There's only you and I
How can I be so calm
How can I be so sure
When I can't feel my body anymore
How can it be
Feeling nothing
And everything

I laid on my side while you slept on your back
My hand resting on your chest
My eyes carefully watching the rise and fall
I never knew I could love someone this much
I kiss your shoulder over and over
You begin to stir and for a moment I feel guilty
Worried that I woke you from peace
Your hand finds mine and you squeeze
No one has ever loved me this much

If only we could stay like this forever
If only the world didn't exist
If only we didn't have so many demons
If only we could stay like this

What if you were the one
The shoulda been
What if soulmates exist
What if I am yours
And you chose darkness
What does that leave me with?

There's something to be said for
Being able to strip down
Physically and emotionally
Walk around without your scars covered
Scream at the top of your lungs
And then look into the eyes of another person
And know that they still love you
They still desire you
They'll still kiss you from head to toe
And hug you tighter while they sleep
It's hard to leave this kind of comfort behind
But it's also devastating when that same person
Will find moments to stick their finger inside
Every single wound you have
Physically and emotionally
Opening you back up, watching you bleed
Reminding you that you're flawed
Imperfect
Unworthy
And it's life changing
To be in this situation and realize that you're not quite sure
What love means
Yet still, instead of strength to leave
You pray today will be a day of comfortability

So many walks in the freezing cold
I'll get you whatever you want
The snow is getting heavy
And our money is almost gone
But I just know that
When you're back on your feet
You're gonna take care of me

Late night screaming matches
You prioritized someone else again
My brain is melting as you repeat the sentence
"She's just a friend"
I feel it in my gut
I know that I'm the fool
I wander out into the brutal winter
And before I even reach my car
I come crawling back to you

Promises whispered
Partnered with the softest of kisses
"I swear to god I'll never hurt you again"
Sobbing in your freezing bedroom
All my hopes riding on you

My hopes shattered before I even got a taste

Driving through Philly's scariest streets
If I can just find you
I know you'll do right by me
You'll get the help, you're going to heal
I just have to bring you home
As soon as you see my face
As soon as you know you're forgiven
You'll surrender to what we have
You'll be better than you've been

Reality has never returned for me
I've lived over two years in a dream
A nightmare, a reckoning
I was destroyed and now I build again
I don't miss or love you, but I still try
To find the good in us, to see the light
And like a broken record I don't want to hear
Buried deep in the bottom of my delusion
"One day he's going to get back on his feet
And he'll do right by me .."

Sometimes
It's easy to ignore the pain
And keep writing you love letters
Painting our past in pretty colors
Pretending things aren't shitty
It's easier to try and right our course
Than it is to try to start a new one

But ours isn't just a course
It's a cycle
A roundabout
We'll always come back to the pain
Always come back to the past
always be shitty

In me you saw
A soul you could take
My weaknesses and insecurities
So clearly on display
I sat drunk on your bed the first night we met
And handed you the keys you would need
To torment me
I opened my soul, spilled every secret
You kept a list of all the ways
You could take advantage of me
You logged every foolish kindness
Marked down every mistake
Knew that you had nothing to offer
Saw everything you could take
I made romance out of that moment
I had never been so willing to share
No one had ever listened so intently
I took a chance on you
I trusted
And I was wrong

They say there's love out there

That makes you feel free

The only love I've known

Has come with chains

Weights

Shackles

There's no love without control

No compassion without compromise

I have fallen into these same habits

Now I'm only willing to love

If I can get something in return

But I demand payment first

Withholding my truth

Avoiding my feelings

"I will love you if you..."

But they never deliver

So I never give

And no one is truly free

I could scream

The cyclone

Every time I think I'm out

I'm sucked back in

I mean it every single time I say

I will never love you again

Yet my ego takes me on the ride

The ups and downs

A useless fight

You say awful things to get me to react

My reaction excites you

Makes you think I give a fuck

I don't

I just so badly want to win

But that's not the way this works

There's no winner here

I lose my cool, my composure, my sanity

And you lose me

It still hurts
You've done things to me
That I'll never recover from
Lies that will follow me
Names that will haunt me
Shit I'll never be able to let go
And yet, the idea
Of you laying next to someone else
Telling them they're beautiful
Watching reruns of Friends
Turns my stomach
The thought that you might
Hug someone else in the middle of the night
Sing our songs
Make our jokes
It all hurts
And oddly enough,
Knowing that you'd only be doing it
To get over me
Only makes it worse

◇◇◇◇◇◇◇◇

Pounds against the walls
Followed by screams
Fighting all of my urges
To run in and see

I can hear things crashing to the floor
I can hear your bruises forming
I can hear our dog barking
Wishing he could transform
Wishing he could get through the door

I hear the evil words he spewed
I can feel you believing them

We sleep with the bedroom door closed
Hoping it'll deter the monster
I sneak out of your room in the morning
Hoping I saved you one more night
Knowing that you save me all the time

We're greeted by laughter
Oh, he's the nice guy today
You run to him with open arms
So relieved to be getting attention
The kind that doesn't cause pain

I can see it in your eyes
You're thinking that maybe he has changed
I feel like I always knew he wouldn't
But I just loved seeing you that way
So I conform
The way the monster wants me to
I'll let him be the good guy today

I wonder how long
We'll maintain this toxic push and pull
How long will it take before
I feel like I've evened out our pain
And hurt you as much as you've hurt me
And if I'm so evolved
And so healed
And so ready to move on
Then why do I keep coming back
Just to hurt you

Constantly craving validation
That I will never get
From someone who will never
Give me closure or praise
I gave everything I have
Depleted myself completely
Because you needed "one more chance"
A hundred different times
I want so badly to move on
I want to heal and not have the urges
To poke at you and demand apologies
Because even when I get them
I know they're not real
And yet I push and push and push
Feeling empty

I never felt good enough
Whether it was drugs
Or other girls
Or another vice
You were always choosing
Something over me
Then I'd get the strength
To walk away
And you'd overload me with promises
And tears
And romantic clichés
I used to tell myself that I deserved better
But I realize now I never believed it
I swore I was staying for love
For comfort
For you
Really I stayed
Because I didn't think
Someone else could love me
And I cringe every day
Thinking about what I allowed
In exchange for occasional affection

I may not be
The awful things you've called me
But I'm certainly not innocent

I was possessed by our attraction
My boundaries dissolved
With them went my rationale

I convinced myself that
Because I knew it was a bad situation
It was okay that I pushed through
It was okay to stay
As long as I was honest about how bad it was

The delusion
Was not all you
I had my own delusions too

I decided it was more important
To love you through your pain
Than it was to protect myself
From the pain you planned to cause

I decided
I stayed
I endured
I chose you

I can be delusional too

I created you in my mind
The first night we spent together
I decided who you were
And who you would be to me
I was wrong

I created expectations you could never meet
You made me promises you could never keep
And together we latched on to something
That should've been short-lived

We were brought together
So that we could change and heal
And then go our separate ways
Instead, we drug it out into a two-year lesson
Now we're left with painful memories
And even more painful mistakes

It took a month of hating you
To realize that I didn't
But it's so painful to accept
That my pain isn't about you

I miss calmer sides of myself
I miss enjoying silence
Without having flashbacks
To moments I was trembling in fear
Without hearing your insults
Repeating over and over
And I know that's confusing
Because you're there
Through all of it
But it isn't about you

It's about what you woke up
What was always laying dormant in me
Silently killing me
And I was so blind I didn't even know
Until you woke the beasts
The pain I associate with you
Was always there
It was caused by many before you
Many more important than you

The universe is using you to heal me

It's sick and twisted
But one of the things I hate the most
Is that I know you'll claim any success I ever have

Any thing I'm able to accomplish
You'll find a way to rearrange it
To proclaim that you got me there
To stick to your version of the story
That I'd be nothing without it you

And the most annoying thing is that
In some ways, it's true

I wouldn't be half the person I am today
If I didn't have to learn how to survive you

◇◇◇◇◇◇◇◇◇

It's not heartbreak
that feels impossible to recover from
It's the betrayal

My heart will heal
My confidence will be restored
Eventually I won't miss you
I'll start to see who you really were
And I'll move on accordingly
One day forgetting that I was even hurt

But the betrayal
That will follow me around forever
The lies
They will always ring in my head

It's not heartbreak
that people get caught up in
It's never knowing who or what to believe

You trust in something
And someone
Only to be let down
So you accept that absolutely any one
Has the ability to let you down
Everyone has the ability to lie
And to mislead

Once you accept that betrayal
Is always on the table
It's nearly impossible
To believe

We both got what we wanted
You got someone to want you
For who you might become
And I found someone who needed me
Promising to change for my love

Over time
This balance can never last
I'll always want the potential you
And you'll always want the me from the past

I spent so much time
Telling myself you loved me
Convincing myself
That it was a reason to stay

Oblivious
To how clear it was
That you didn't respect me
And what's the point
Of love without respect

You woke my demons
The ones I thought I had killed off
I had myself convinced
That I had healed
But instead, everything was buried
Sleeping
Waiting to be kissed
So they could rise again and
Force me to grow
And force me to live

There are people I have touched
That I never think of
And people I've never heard speak
But listen for at all times
There are paths I crossed so very briefly
It's a wonder I'm able to recall details
And then moments that stretch over years
Yet, they never cross my mind
It's so strange what the heart keeps
And what logic pushes away
Sometimes we forget
So that we can protect ourselves
And sometimes we remember
For the same

How was I to know
You'd never get better

How naive was I to think
My love could push you through

How foolish to believe
You'd heal
Just by loving me

How presumptuous
To think I was stronger
Than any of your past lovers

How blind did I have to be
To think you saw
Something worthy

And how damaged is my heart
That I'm still putting all the blame
On me

I spent years
Begging
Pleading
For you to get help

I nursed you through illness
Held you while you cried
Excused every ugly thing
That you said and did to me

"He's not well,
But one day he will be"

Nothing
No progress
No change

And now that I have closed my heart
And abandoned all faith
You want to talk of love and healing
And I just want you to go away

We were so volatile
I had no choice but to leave
I stayed
I tried
I waited
And every single time
You made a fool of me

Yet now that I have found the strength
To close the door and move on
You're able to act as if I'm breaking your heart
As if I did something wrong

While I was busy believing in you
All you ever did was let me down

You don't give me things
Or do favors
To be kind
Or to make me feel special
You commit acts of questionable kindness
So that you have something to hold over my head
Something to take away
It's never about me
It's always about control
You give
Only to take
While I gave
And gave
Hoping to keep you

I used to melt when you kissed me
I would shake at every touch
I was genuinely moved by you
I still adore your crooked smile
And am captured by your telling eyes
But I don't remember a time
I cringed from being happily overwhelmed
Instead of being unnerved
And yet here I am
Checking my phone
Searching my heart
Dissecting my memory reel
Fooling myself

Mirrors
What a trick they play
Loving reflection in the evening
And a monster during the day

In you I found a mirror
I felt different
Each time that I glared
Sometimes I got answers
Other times, questions
But it would unfold the more I stared
No sense to be made
Of what is in front of me
And still I keep my eyes fixed
No good can come from loving you
And still, I just can't help it

The sun shines confidently
But my view is so gray
I take deep breaths
Steady my brain
"Everything is going to be okay.."
And then it washes over me
Because trauma comes in waves
Your name appears
And my heart stops
I know it doesn't matter what you say
But my addiction to you
Creates curiosity
And I read it anyway
Your tone is not hard to decipher
The demon is out to play
I wish I didn't recognize him so easily
But this is the reality of my days
To reply or not reply
Just another game I play
"Maybe I can love him through it"
The fool in me begins to say
Logic and emotion
Waging war inside my brain
If I ignore you, I'll get stronger

But can strength be maintained?

I miss you

I miss you

I miss you

The only line you say

A whole week gone

I don't respond

To the nine "I miss yous" a day

There has to be more

I scream to myself

He has to have more to say

But by day 6, I'm broken down

And I know it doesn't matter either way

...and so I entertain

Empty words and promises

Your potential on display

My guilt and shame piling up

Just walk the fuck away

Life

Hands down

Harder than death

And losing someone

Who is still alive

Is endless suffering

We know where the dead go

We know how to be with them

But the living that we've lost

Those ties are never cut

They're just always around

Tugging at us

But out of reach

It's harder to mourn the living

They're not buried

Sometimes when I'm sitting alone at night
Giving way to the silence
Hoping for peace
I imagine your hand around my throat
And you won't stop until I can't breathe
I imagine choking on my own blood
While you yell and spit at me
And you see, the thing is
I didn't imagine it
I'm remembering

And that's why I always believe people
When I hear them speak of ghosts
You're still haunting me

Haunted

I always thought people were being dramatic

Claiming their skeletons were lurking nearby

Afraid to speak

To love

To live

Always waiting for their past to unmask itself

And drag them back

Back to the long nights

Back to the aches and pains

Back to the lying, the cheating, the stealing

Back to having to explain

"Just let it go and it will let go of you"

The rebuttal to resistance

But now that you're a ghost of mine

I understand how more delicate people

Weren't able to live like this

I sit
And try to think of a time
When
The good outweighed the pain
I search our entire relationship
And I can't fuckin find it
I can't find one single
"Remember when..."
That isn't connected to a
"How fuckin could you"
It's all ugly now
Every trace of you and I
Every touch
Every kiss
Every memory
Takes me to a bad place
And yet here I am
Flipping through our pages
Forever determined
There just has to be good in there somewhere
There has to be a reason
that I'm so committed
To living in the dark

I'll love you for the rest of my life

Though most days I wish it wasn't true

I'll always wonder what would have happened

If I had gotten the healthy version of you

I'll wonder how you would've loved me

If you were able to do so without worry

And I wonder if we could've made it work

I wonder if you would've still hurt me

It used to break my heart

Remembering that we'd never be together

But now

it just puts me at ease

I bet we were lovers in a past life
I bet we waged wars and came out on top
But I bet we fought for different sides
Subconsciously being
The others worst enemy
I can't love someone who won't let me in
And you won't barge in without knowing I love you

Aren't you tired yet?
You've spent the better years of your life
Hiding behind a mask
Speaking in riddles and lies
Medicating your pain
Being led by fear and pride
How can you not want more?

It's at the point that
I trust you more than I trust myself
You treat me terribly
And disregard me completely
But at least you're consistent
I love myself some days
And manage to power through
And on other days I'm a sucker
To me and you
But I can rely on you to hurt me
It's the one constant I can count on
But me? I'm a wild card
Am I in, am I out?

Loveless.

When you're unhappy in a relationship

People assume its loveless

If you're treated badly

People assume its loveless

"You should just leave if he doesn't love you"

OK. But he does

Passionately

Obsessively

When the lights are out and he's planted at my feet

Bowing on his knees

Professing

When he brings my coffee to my bed side

When he wakes at 3am to grab me Tylenol for my aching bones

When he phones just to say I'm beautiful

When he holds my head in his hands and softly kisses away the pain

When he flirts with me on a Tuesday afternoon

When he consumes my soul with his

And truly makes me believe

That I'm the only woman alive

Loveless, you say

"It must not be real" they claim

You see..
I'm not fighting for someone who doesn't love ME
His anger
His words
His disregard
His frustration

His absence
His self-medication
These are not the characteristics of someone who doesn't love me
with all he has
He just doesn't love himself
And it's beautiful to believe
That loving him back
Can make him see his worth

It's not easy to love the devil

He is combative

And pushes you away

But it's not easy to leave him either

He creates such good reasons

To make you stay

We go days without speaking
And I fall in love with the calm
Or so I think...
But then it occurs to me
How little you must care
That you haven't even tried
And just like that
I need to hear your voice
I need to hear your reactions
They're awful
You yell and scream
And put me down
And you'd think
This would make me stop
"How little he must care"
But instead now I'm fighting
Harassing
Questioning everything you say
Breaking my own heart
While you belittle me
Or even worse
While you ignore me
And when the moment passes

And I come to
Breaking through my rage blackout
I hate myself for being weak
I hate myself for thriving off chaos
Why couldn't I just enjoy the calm
Instead of constantly forcing a storm?
I'm my own worst enemy
And you're my weapon of choice

I don't fear evil
I have slept with
And loved evil
Until my soul started to turn
I have defended and desired the devil
I even taught him a thing or two
It's calm that makes me tremble
Silence and stability
They rock my very core
I need the chaos
I need the drama
I'm accustomed to the evil
It's the unknown angels
That I fear

Sometimes I wish

I never got strong

Wish I was still blinded

By your forced charm

Wish I still believed your lies

It was blissful

Briefly

Not knowing any better

Not knowing what love should look like

We always say that the people that have wrong us don't
deserve our love
But maybe we're going about it wrong…

They don't deserve our energy,
Our time,
Our clenched jaws or tears
They don't deserve explanations
Or platforms to give their own

But love?
Who are we to decide?
Who are we to pick and choose kindness?

⬦⬦⬦⬦⬦⬦⬦

I used to ask why you loved me
And you never had answers
At least not that
Reflected my character
Only about how I made you feel
What I could do for you

That's always when I felt the emptiest

Listening to you explain
How my love served you
While I faced the reality
Of how little I was loved

At first, I felt a puncture
And I couldn't believe you were stabbing me

But then I felt the release
All the pain draining out of me

I can breathe

…and we thought you had killed me

I study your frozen face
All I see is pain
I know time is of the essence
I know you want to stay
The pressure is apparent
Though I'm careful not to push
I watch your eyes lighten
As you give me a serious look
And suddenly the world is brighter
As a smile finds your lips
Your face opens wider
And the mood between us flips
Back and forth we continue this
Never saying a word
I lay a hand upon your shoulder
And all my thoughts are heard
I feel your glance shoot through me
A tightness forms in my core
We still haven't said a thing
But I don't wonder anymore
It's as if I'm finally seeing through you
And so, my confidence, it spikes
I've been waiting for something to happen
Been waiting for a sign
But when I'm sitting at your side
Doing nothing is alright
I know we'll get our time

And I stood
At the top of the world
Hands on my hips
Deep breaths
Wanting nothing more than to trust you
To believe you
To need you
Deep, deep breaths
Who are we?
What do we want?
My head spinning
Feelings changing over and over
Why can't I quit you...?
Why can't I commit to you?
Can't seem to let you go
Or let you in

If it wasn't this ending

It would be another

The only good I'll take of you

Moments we were lovers

Clinging on, literally

I look back now and I wonder

How I convinced myself

To turn a blind eye

To take that hour drive

To answer the unknown numbers

Time and time again

I don't think I was ever happy

That's what hurts the most

I knew I was miserable

And I put you first anyway

I never knew what love was

And neither did you

But our fucked up versions of it

Fit together so well

"Today…"
"Today, I'll be better"
I'll keep my emotions in check
And politely speak my mind
I won't allow you to misbehave
But I won't stifle your attempts
At making me feel loved
And then I fail
In so many ways
I bring up the past
Your tone threatens me
Your phone brings out my insecurities
You turn me down for sex
I lose my cool
Punches thrown
You gracefully back off
How are you so calm?
It infuriates me more
"you're fuckin nuts"
"you need help"
I do. I wish I could say it.
I do
I do need help
I need your kindness
Your reassurance
I need a promise of change
I need your gratitude

I need your understanding
I need your help
I need you to hear me
Instead, I leave
Screaming more expletives
Directed at your ego
Determined to inflict pain
We promise it's over
Then we do it again
I apologize
When I'm wrong
When I hurt you
When I go too far
I apologize
When you're wrong
When you hurt me
When you go too far
How dare I provoke you
"cry it out"
"cry it out and be done"
I tell myself as I pick an angrier song
And then I lose more pieces of myself
Waiting for your attention
All day long
…and then I get it
This time I'll be better

Days like these happen so often between us
It's almost painful to apologize
It hurts to come to grips
With all the awful things I have said
The awful things I claim to have done
It's painful to acknowledge
The lengths I would go to, to hurt you
Especially since
It destroys me to hurt you
But this competition we've created
This never-ending need
To hurt the other person first
Before they hurt us worse
I have found it more important lately
To be the winner
Than to be the bigger person
Because for so, so long
You pushed me and pushed me and pushed
That I don't even know if you hear me
When I am saying nice things
I feel that you're only listening to me
When I'm tearing you down
I want you to know
That since day one
I have fantasized of ways
To love your pain away
But unfortunately for me
Since day one
You have always found ways
To make me feel bad
For loving you so much
And then there's moments
When I get a small glimpse
Of how much you claim to love me
And for seconds, for milliseconds
I believe that you actually do

But then my brain fires off
A million different tricks you could be playing
A million different lies you've already told
So many things you need me for
And needing me
Is not the same as wanting me
Part of the reason I command you away
Is because I cant bear to hurt you anymore

It drains me of all the good in me
That I have worked so hard to preserve
But on the other side of that
I'm compelled to command you away
Because every version of wanting to love you
Just seems to hurt
These goodbyes are so often temporary
Because I worry and I obsess
Is he eating? Is he breathing? Is he okay?
Is he aching? Does he miss me?
Has his pain gone away?
Did he replace me already…?
With someone who doesn't deserve him?
Has he been hiding her for months
And the joke has been on me on purpose?
Have I loved him so powerfully
That now he wants to be better for someone else?
Have I damaged him so, so deeply
That he doesn't think anything is worth being felt?
So many questions
I nag myself all night and day
So many answers
That will never come
All I wish for us is peace
But I don't think that exists if we remain
All I wish for you is happiness
But all I do is take your happiness

You deemed me a cold hearted bitch
Claimed I had built my walls so high
There's no way you could get in
And love me

There weren't simple enough words
For me to explain to you
That you had actually built those walls
You blocked your own way
With lies, absence, abuse…

And cold hearted bitch?
Far, far from it
But if I reacted emotionally
To every thing you did that hurt me
I'd never get anything else done

When we were together

I thought I knew what love was

I didn't understand why

I couldn't get out of bed in the morning

Why I couldn't fall asleep at night

Why I was defensive at every comment

And a puppet in my own life

I couldn't make sense of the emptiness

How could we be in love

And me be so broken?

It's so strange, isn't it?

How you can be completely shattered

Depressed

Checked out of your own existence

And yet still believe

You are experiencing love

I laid in your bed with my eyes closed tight
Fists clenched, faking sleep with all my might
It occurred to me that I didn't feel safe
I was ready every second to defend myself

You open your mouth to speak
My walls go up around me
I beg my soul to keep quiet
Instead of reaching into my bag of passiveness

You say the words I wanted to hear
This morning before you waged a war
You express feelings I was longing for
Before you decided your ego needed a stroke

You call me cold and calculated
That I don't know how to love
But any time I try it out on you
You use it to level the playing field
And by the time you unlock my cage
I'm no longer the tender heart I was
When we started out the day

Curled in your sheets with gritted teeth
It occurs to me that I don't feel safe
You reach out to find me
I roll away
You say you miss me, you say you'll change
Brick by brick I raise my guard
Yet hour by hour, I stay

I feel uneasiness in my bones
Like I could crumble at any minute
My eyes are stinging
My cheeks are read
Years and years and years of repetition
Here I am
Right back in it

It feels so different this time
As if the end might be near
And I can't tell by my racing heart
If it's an end that features you
Physically existing here

I remind myself to take deep breaths
But my inhales are being blocked
Tingles up and down my skin
The what-ifs just wont stop

I wish I would've said I love you
Though I know it would have fallen silent
I wish you would have made eye contact
But I guess you didn't want me knowing
What is really on your mind

I'm afraid to fall asleep
Worried about what tomorrow might bring
Reluctant to stay awake
It would be nice to escape
I pray you're finally finding peace
Whether it be by grace or by harm
May the road you choose be the welcoming one
I hear the third time is a charm

Every time you threaten to "be done" with me

I love you a little bit less

It comes off in tiny little pieces

But I imagine that one day

It's going to run out

All of the love will have flaked off of me

And there won't be any attachment left

There will be no reminder you were ever here

And sometimes I don't know if

I'm always dreading that day

Or always praying for it

The thrashing of the wind keeps me awake

It screams out for attention

Ripping things one way

And then tossing them another

Behaving so violently

When it only longs to be free

It reminds me of you

I don't know where to go from here
Daily conversations with a stranger
That I have loved for over two years
How can I know everything about you
And not know a single thing

I suppose it's how we find the balance
Similar to the way
I love you to your very core
And hate you from deep in mine

You screamed and screamed into the phone
Enraged that I don't care
Calling from another hospital bed
More lies about why you're there
My composure is killing you
You prefer when I'm unhinged
You prefer when I'm afraid to lose you
While I'm hoping you disappear again

I wish you no harm
No foul play
I wish you could heal
And mean the things you say
But this ride has nothing to offer me
And I'm tired of being in pain
You blame me
You threaten me
You point fingers
Then you relentless chase
Once I escape

I no longer wish to play

I lose my will

I lose my strength

Then you crumble

And I'm strong again

I stay solid

To keep you in one piece

You deny my abilities

You talk down to me

I'm your last life line

Yet you push me away on your good days

Scream for me when you're suffering

Abandon me when you're floating

Lucky you

Release in your veins

Hardly any memories

No self-awareness to your name

Lucky you

Loved by someone like me

But I've seen luck like this before

And it always runs out

You're the rush that damages my very being
The shove that simply breaks my heart in two
And you're the ache I can't help but feeling
I'm not sure I'll ever get over you

I crash onto the floor
Harder than you crash into me
I'm the victim every single time
You use me so carelessly
But always with my permission
I'm walking away from what doesn't want me
But even I can't support my decision

I had hoped we'd take these secrets to our graves
But I've witnessed you give them away
I've heard your laugh that follows
I cannot stand you being so close
You're still my favorite place

You adore my vulnerability
You always seem to get what you want
You're the only thing that has ever given me any stability
You're the reason that all my strength is gone

There's no way I can explain what I would do to get to you

And no words to express the way it feels to know that it wouldn't matter

These memories crack under the pressure of your anger towards me

My heart aches knowing your potential to cause my whole world to shatter

No longer can I seem to pretend that I've put you behind me

It's disgusting the way you always brought out the best in me

So pathetic that you're the one guilty of wrecking me

I'm a lost cause for even allowing myself to admit this at all

I am awakened by our rise, amazed by the way I've loved you

I am completely destroyed by our crash, crushed by our fall

every heart can feel the pain in every one of these lines, I'm coming down

unfolded and exposed for the mess that I am & it's all my fault

I drag on reluctantly, day after day just hoping that maybe

you'll hear how well I'm doing and come back to ruin my progress

I'll perfect my strong front if it means that you'll return & pull me under

I'd face the ending all over again if it meant one more real moment with you

I'm beyond emotional, I'm trapped by our past, so confused with myself

so surrounded and haunted by the fact that there will never be anyone else

I have "one more chance"

Myself through two years

"One more try, there's nothing to lose"

That's what I tell myself

When you beg and plead

"What is there to lose?"

Now I think about the days

The weeks

The months

Time spent crying

Time spent sleeping off the pain

Time I've spent lying to defend you

"What is there to lose…?"

Just the rest of my life I suppose

I wonder what that's worth to you

I have blocked so much of us out

Sometimes I stumble upon a memory
And am embarrassed by what I've allowed

It really makes the fact that
I always seem to prolong our time together
So much more confusing

I wrote my final plea
On a dirty white sheet
The one we all signed
When you turned eighteen
You blew out candles
I was wishing you were wishing for me
The universe kept bringing us back together
And reality keep ripping us away
11 years have passed
And I still think of you today
I think of your hunched shoulders
As you cried near my totaled car
I think of you on the floral couch
The night I broke your heart
I think of your life now
And I pray that you're complete
And though I'd never wish you confusion
I still hope you think of me
But "what ifs" are risky
And one change to the past changes everything
I guess I just didn't realize then
That the words I scribbled years ago
Would still stand true

However far away, I will always love you

Swift movements to describe your guilt
Hit my chest like tidal waves
Taking me to the floor
So now I can look up to you
And it's all you've been asking for
These blows though, I'll take them any day
As opposed to the way you talk to me
And rip apart everything I have convinced myself
It is okay to be

I'll rebuild myself, I'll recover
But I will never put my trust in anyone else
I will change, I will be better
And I will always be by myself

Right on the edge of a cliff with your hands on my shoulders
Push me now and love me no further
I tuck my head under bracing for the crash
Instead you tighten your grip and pull me back

I forgive you
There's not much else to do these days

Your threats, they come down heavy

They land real hard, ending every hope and dream

Stomping my aching heart

And everything I always thought I would do

You promised me I'd be the best one

And now you tie strings to me

Changing my directions, hating my plans

Who am I to try and understand

I'll never be who you want me to be

Because your vision is always changing

So I change the way I see you

Change my eyes, change my needs

You change your ways, you change me

And everything you think you know about me

You're probably very wrong

But I know your intentions were good

And you, you're just misunderstood